FIELD GUIDES

BIRDS OF PREY

Andrea Debbink

Abdo Reference

An Imprint of Abdo Publishing | abdobooks.com

CONTENTS

Falcons

Falconets

Kestrels

Osprey and Secretary Bird

Typical Owls

Barn Owls and Others

WHAT ARE BIRDS OF PREY?

Birds of prey hunt, scavenge, and feed on vertebrate animals such as fish, mammals, and other birds. They have hooked beaks and usually have powerful feet with sharp talons that they use to grasp prey. Some birds of prey are active during the day while others are active only at night.

BIRDS OF PREY CATEGORIES

There are more than 500 bird of prey species in the world. All are divided into two main groups. Within the two groups, birds are categorized into families and species based on behaviors, habitats, and physical characteristics.

- Nocturnal: Birds of prey that are active at night include typical owls and barn owls.

- Diurnal: Birds of prey that hunt during the day are divided into many separate categories, including bazas, eagles, hawks, harriers, kites, Old World vultures, New World vultures, caracaras, falcons, falconets, kestrels, the osprey, and the secretary bird.

BIRDS OF PREY IDENTIFICATION

Birds of prey can be difficult to identify because unlike songbirds, they're often seen by humans only at a distance. There are also many similarities in the shapes and color patterns among birds of prey species that can make them difficult to tell apart. In general, birds of prey appear in a limited range of muted colors, including white, brown, black, rust, and gray. Yet there are other factors that can affect the colors and patterns of an individual bird:

- Age: Young birds have different colors and patterns than adult birds of the same species.

- Sex: In some species, such as bald eagles, males and females can look nearly identical. But in other species, males and females have different colors and markings.

- Morphs: Some bird species, such as red-tailed hawks, have two or more main color variations, called morphs.

- Season: Bird feathers wear out over time, so all birds, including birds of prey, regularly molt. This means birds shed old feathers and grow new ones. Depending on the species, this can happen in a season or take several years. While it's molting, a bird may have different colors and patterns than others of its species.

In this book, birds are described according to their most common adult coloration and pattern. In addition to a bird's color pattern and shape, there are some other things to consider when identifying a bird of prey:

- Size: The average height and weight of each bird species.

- Range: The geographic area where the bird species lives in the world. If the species migrates, its range will change during the year.

- Habitat: The type of environment where a bird species lives, such as a wetland, forest, or other ecosystem.

- Diet: What the bird usually eats. All birds of prey are carnivores, but some species are hunters while others, such as vultures, are scavengers.

Tab shows the bird of prey category.

TYPICAL OWLS

BARRED OWL *(STRIX VARIA)*

The barred owl is a very vocal bird that makes a range of sounds. It cackles and caws, and its most common call ~~sounds~~ like "who-cooks-for-you, ... are stocky birds. They ... acing, dark eyes; and ... wn and white with various ~~streaks~~

The bird of prey's common name appears here.

Images show the bird of prey.

HOW TO SPOT

Size: 17 to 19.5 inches (43 to 50 cm) long; 1 to 2.3 pounds (0.5 to 1 kg)

Range: North America

Habitat: Forests, temperate rain forests, and cypress swamps

Diet: Small mammals, birds, amphibians, reptiles, and insects

How to Spot boxes give information about the bird of prey's size, range, habitat, and diet.

88

6

BLAKISTON'S FISH O

(KETUPA BLAKISTONI)

The Blakiston's fish owl is the biggest owl species in the world. It can weigh up to 10 pounds (4.5 kg) and has an incredible 6-foot (1.8-m) wingspan. These birds have long, brown feathers that look like shaggy fur. They also have dramatic ear tufts that look like ears. Unlike other owls, they're not silent flyers. That doesn't matter much, though, because their main prey is fish.

HOW TO SPOT

Size: 23 to 28 inches (58 to 71 cm) long;
(3.2 to 4.5 kg)
Range: Japan, Russia, and China
Habitat: Old-growth forests near rivers
Diet: Fish, crustaceans, birds, and frogs

FUN FACT
Male and female Blakiston's fish owls perform their calls in a duet.

AN ENDANGERED OWL
Blakiston's fish owls are endangered. They live only i
few remote areas of old-growth forests in China, Jap
and far-eastern Russia. They tend to avoid contact
with people.

89

The bird of prey's scientific name appears here.

The paragraph gives information about the bird of prey.

Fun Facts give interesting information about the bird of prey.

Sidebars provide additional information about the topic.

AFRICAN CUCKOO-HAWK
(AVICEDA CUCULOIDES)

The African cuckoo-hawk is a type of raptor called a baza. Its crested head, back, and wings are grayish brown, and its chest is barred. This medium-sized raptor is a weak flyer and spends a lot of time perched in trees, where it watches for prey on the ground.

HOW TO SPOT

Size: 15 to 17 inches (38 to 43 cm) long; around 0.5 pounds (0.23 kg)

Range: Africa

Habitat: Savannas and forests near rivers and coasts

Diet: Lizards, grasshoppers, crabs, fish, and small birds

FUN FACT

Birds in the baza family are sometimes called cuckoo hawks. That's because they're the same size and shape as the common cuckoo, and they drop down on their prey like hawks.

BLACK BAZA *(AVICEDA LEUPHOTES)*

Black bazas are raptors with mostly black feathers and wings that flap slowly in flight. These birds have crested heads, a white band across their upper chests, and white-and-brown striped feathers along their sides. When it's not breeding season, black bazas can be very social birds, flying and roosting together in large flocks.

HOW TO SPOT

Size: 11 to 13.7 inches (28 to 35 cm) long; 0.37 to 0.5 pounds (0.17 to 0.23 kg)

Range: Southeast Asia, China, eastern Himalayas, and northeast India

Habitat: Deciduous or tropical forests

Diet: Large insects, lizards, and tree frogs

AFRICAN FISH EAGLE
(HALIAEETUS VOCIFER)

African fish eagles are a common sight along Africa's waterways. They're often perched in trees near rivers or lakes because their main food source is fish. African fish eagles have bright-white heads and chests, and part of their wings, backs, and tail feathers are dark reddish brown. They have a distinctive call that sounds like a yelp. They make this sound when perched or flying.

HOW TO SPOT

Size: 25 to 30 inches (63 to 77 cm) long; 4 to 8 pounds (1.8 to 3.6 kg)

Range: Africa

Habitat: Along rivers, lakes, wetlands, and estuaries

Diet: Fish, carrion, birds, small mammals, and reptiles

WHAT ARE EAGLES?

Eagles are powerful birds of prey known for their strength and size. They have hooked beaks, strong talons, and long, rounded wings for soaring. There are more than 60 eagle species in the world, and nearly all of them eat live prey—from rodents and nestlings to fish and snakes.

BALD EAGLE
(HALIAEETUS LEUCOCEPHALUS)

The bald eagle was close to extinction in the mid-1900s, but today it's more common throughout North America. It is usually seen in tall trees along waterways. While it prefers fish, the bald eagle is also a scavenger and eats many different things. It will also steal food from other raptors. The bald eagle has a white head, yellow beak, and dark-brown body. It's a very large bird—the second-largest bird of prey in North America.

HOW TO SPOT

Size: 28 to 38 inches (71 to 97 cm) long; 6.6 to 14 pounds (3 to 6.4 kg)

Range: North America

Habitat: Along rivers, lakes, wetlands, and estuaries

Diet: Fish, carrion, reptiles, amphibians, crustaceans, and mammals

FUN FACT
In 1782, the US Congress chose the bald eagle as the national emblem of the United States.

THE EAGLE'S COMEBACK

The comeback of the bald eagle is one of the biggest environmental success stories in the United States. By the middle of the 1900s, the bald eagle was endangered because of hunting and the use of chemical pesticides. There were fewer than 500 pairs of breeding bald eagles throughout the country. But thanks to environmental protection laws passed in the 1960s and 1970s, the bald eagle population rebounded to more than 300,000 by 2021.

BATELEUR *(TERATHOPIUS ECAUDATUS)*

The bateleur is an eagle that has short tail feathers. It also has contrasting patches of color on its mostly black body. These patches of color are on the bird's sides and back. They can range from gray to light reddish brown. Adult bateleurs have scarlet-red faces and feet. While these birds will hunt live prey, they prefer to scavenge carrion.

FUN FACT

Bateleurs can spend up to 80 percent of the day soaring in the skies looking for carcasses on the ground.

HOW TO SPOT

Size: 22 to 28 inches (56 to 71 cm) long; 4 to 6 pounds (1.8 to 2.7 kg)

Range: Africa

Habitat: Savannas and open forests

Diet: Carrion, small mammals, birds, and reptiles

BLACK EAGLE *(ICTINAETUS MALAIENSIS)*

Black eagles can be seen soaring over forests in Southeast Asia. These large raptors appear all-black from a distance, but they are actually dark brown with faint tan stripes on some of their feathers. The bird's beak and feet are yellow. In flight, the broad wings of black eagles have distinctive feathers that stick out from the ends, resembling fingers. This species is a mostly silent hunter.

HOW TO SPOT

Size: 25.5 to 31 inches (65 to 79 cm) long; 2 to 3.5 pounds (0.9 to 1.6 kg)

Range: Southeast Asia

Habitat: Forested hills and mountains

Diet: Birds, eggs, lizards, small mammals, and bats

BROWN SNAKE EAGLE
(CIRCAETUS CINEREUS)

The brown snake eagle gets its name from the main food it eats: snakes. These medium-sized eagles swoop down at snakes and kill them on the ground. Then they often bring the snakes back to their nests. Brown snake eagles are covered in various shades of brown feathers. Like other raptors, their feet are covered in a layer of scales. These protect the brown snake eagle from snake bites.

FUN FACT

There are six species of snake eagles, and they all eat mainly snakes. Some even consume venomous types of snakes, such as cobras.

HOW TO SPOT

Size: 28 to 31 inches (71 to 79 cm) long; 3 to 5.5 pounds (1.4 to 2.5 kg)

Range: Africa

Habitat: Savannas, open forests, and semidesert areas

Diet: Snakes, lizards, and rodents

CROWNED EAGLE
(STEPHANOAETUS CORONATUS)

Crowned eagles have gray, brown, and white patterned feathers with stripes across their tails and the undersides of their wings. Their legs are covered in a thick layer of white-and-brown feathers, and their feet are yellow. The crowned eagle has a crest, but it usually lays flat against the bird's head. This raptor lives in dense forests in Africa, where it hunts monkeys in the treetops.

HOW TO SPOT

Size: 31 to 39 inches (79 to 99 cm) long; 6 to 10 pounds (2.7 to 4.5 kg)
Range: Africa
Habitat: Forests
Diet: Mammals and rodents

GOLDEN EAGLE *(AQUILA CHRYSAETOS)*

The powerful golden eagle has a large range and can be found across the northern hemisphere in various habitats. Golden eagles prefer to live in remote areas away from human developments. These birds have brown feathers with golden-brown feathers around their necks. They feed on small mammals but have been known to hunt larger mammals such as mountain goats, seals, and coyotes.

FUN FACT

Although golden eagles are solitary birds, they will sometimes work together and hunt in pairs.

HOW TO SPOT

Size: 28 to 39 inches (71 to 99 cm) long; 6.6 to 13 pounds (3 to 6 kg)

Range: Africa, Asia, Europe, and North America

Habitat: Grasslands, deserts, forests, mountains, and hills

Diet: Mammals, birds, reptiles, and fish

HARPY EAGLE *(HARPIA HARPYJA)*

Harpy eagles are very large and rare eagles that spend most of their time in the canopies of tropical evergreen forests. Despite their large wings, these eagles rarely soar. Harpy eagles have gray heads, gray or black wings and backs, and white chests. Although they have a diverse diet, harpy eagles prefer to eat medium-sized mammals such as monkeys and sloths.

HOW TO SPOT

Size: 34 to 42 inches (86 to 107 cm) long; 9 to 20 pounds (4.1 to 9.1 kg)

Range: Central and South America

Habitat: Tropical evergreen forests

Diet: Mammals and birds

LESSER FISH EAGLE
(HALIAEETUS HUMILIS)

The lesser fish eagle is the smallest fish eagle species, weighing less than 2 pounds (0.9 kg). Its small head and neck are a dark, streaky gray. The bird's wings and back are grayish brown, and its legs and lower belly are white. This small eagle feeds exclusively on fish and lives along forested rivers and streams in Asia.

HOW TO SPOT

Size: 20 to 27 inches (51 to 69 cm) long; less than 2 pounds (0.9 kg)
Range: Southeast Asia
Habitat: Forested rivers and streams
Diet: Fish

FUN FACT

The bottoms of the lesser fish eagle's toes have a rough layer of spikes. This helps the bird grip slippery fish. Other fish-eating species also have this feature.

MARTIAL EAGLE
(POLEMAETUS BELLICOSUS)

The martial eagle is one of the largest eagle species in Africa. It has a wingspan of up to 7 feet (2 m). With these large wings, martial eagles spend most of their time soaring as they search for prey on the ground below. They can spot prey up to 4 miles (6.4 km) away. This bird is mostly brown with a small crest at the back of its head. Its underbelly and legs are white with small, brown spots.

HOW TO SPOT

Size: 31 to 38 inches (79 to 97 cm) long; 6 to 13 pounds (2.7 to 5.9 kg)

Range: Africa

Habitat: Savannas, grasslands, shrublands, and deserts

Diet: Large birds, lizards, and small mammals

PALLAS'S FISH EAGLE *(HALIAEETUS LEUCORYPHUS)*

The Pallas's fish eagle lives near fresh water throughout Asia, but it's an uncommon bird even in its natural habitat. Like all fish eagles, it eats mainly fish but will also eat other small animals such as birds and reptiles. The Pallas's fish eagle has a reddish-brown body. When it soars, a broad, white stripe is visible on the underside of each wing.

HOW TO SPOT

Size: 28 to 33 inches (71 to 84 cm) long; 4 to 8 pounds (1.8 to 3.6 kg)
Range: Asia
Habitat: Rivers, lakes, and wetlands
Diet: Fish, birds, rodents, reptiles, and frogs

FUN FACT
If an eagle species feeds mainly on fish, it's considered to be a fish eagle or sea eagle.

STELLER'S SEA EAGLE
(HALIAEETUS PELAGICUS)

Steller's sea eagles live where they can find a ready supply of fish, especially Pacific salmon. They hunt along the Pacific coast of Asia or near the mouths of rivers and are rarely seen inland. Steller's sea eagles build their nests in the tops of tall trees or on rocky cliffs. This huge bird is mostly dark brown with white shoulders and legs, and it has a white tail that is wedged-shaped. The Steller's sea eagle has bright-yellow feet and a large, hooked beak that's also bright yellow.

HOW TO SPOT

Size: 33 to 41 inches (84 to 104 cm) long; 11 to 20 pounds (5 to 9.1 kg)

Range: Eastern Asia

Habitat: Sea coasts and rivers

Diet: Fish, carrion, and small mammals

FAR FROM HOME

Sometimes a bird flies far from its usual range and continues to wander. Scientists call this behavior vagrancy. In 2020, a lone Steller's sea eagle set a new record for this behavior. The eagle was spotted in Alaska, about 4,700 miles (7,560 km) away from its normal range in Asia.

TAWNY EAGLE *(AQUILA RAPAX)*

The tawny eagle is a bird of prey that prefers open, dry habitats such as plains and steppes. These birds range in color from pale tan to dark brown. They have dark feathers on their wings and tails, along with light-colored bars on their wings. Tawny eagles have short legs that are covered in a thick layer of feathers. Since they will eat carrion, tawny eagles are sometimes seen foraging at garbage dumps or landfills within their range. Tawny eagles may mate for life. Their mating display takes place in the sky, and a female and male may even lock their claws together while flying.

HOW TO SPOT

Size: 24 to 29 inches (61 to 74 cm) long; 3.5 to 6.6 pounds (1.6 to 3 kg)

Range: Africa and Asia

Habitat: Open woodlands, semidesert, and steppes

Diet: Carrion, mammals, birds, and lizards

WHITE-BELLIED SEA EAGLE
(HALIAEETUS LEUCOGASTER)

Like most eagles, the white-bellied sea eagle is an opportunistic feeder. Although it can and will hunt live prey such as seabirds, fruit bats, and fish, it also scavenges. This sea eagle can be seen foraging through trash bins, looking for carrion along the tide line, and even following dolphins to steal some of their prey. The white-bellied sea eagle has a white body and head, and its wings are dark gray.

HOW TO SPOT

Size: 30 to 33 inches (76 to 84 cm) long; 5 to 6.6 pounds (2.3 to 3 kg)

Range: Southeast Asia, India, Australia, and Tasmania

Habitat: Coasts and waterways

Diet: Mammals, birds, fish, carrion, and crustaceans

FUN FACT
Because of its large size and hunting skills, the white-bellied sea eagle can attack prey that's as large as a swan.

AFRICAN MARSH HARRIER
(CIRCUS RANIVORUS)

African marsh harriers, like all harriers, have streamlined bodies with slender wings. When perched, they appear to be completely brown. When they fly, it is clear that the undersides of their wings have bold, brown-and-white stripes. True to their name, African marsh harriers are common in marshes across southern Africa.

HOW TO SPOT

Size: 17 to 19 inches (43 to 48 cm) long; 0.9 to 1.3 pounds (0.4 to 0.6 kg)

Range: Southern Africa

Habitat: Marshes

Diet: Small rodents, birds, eggs, frogs, and insects

WHAT IS A HARRIER?

Harriers are a type of hawk. They often have plain coloring, small beaks, and long tails and legs. While hunting, they soar low over marshes and meadows. Instead of nesting in trees, harriers make their homes in tall grasses or marshes. Females can lay between four and six blue or white eggs.

COMMON BLACK HAWK
(BUTEOGALLUS ANTHRACINUS)

Common black hawks live along rivers and streams in Central and South America. They are also known to migrate to southern areas of North America. The common black hawk appears to be completely black when stationary. But when it flies, a wide, white band can be seen on the underside of its tail. In addition, the undersides of its wings are mottled brown.

HOW TO SPOT

Size: 17 to 22 inches (43 to 56 cm) long; 1.8 to 2.6 pounds (0.8 to 1.2 kg)

Range: Southern North America, Central America, and northern South America

Habitat: Forested rivers and streams, wetlands, coastal plains, and mountain streams

Diet: Large insects, reptiles, crustaceans, fish, and carrion

FUN FACT
In the northern parts of their range, common black hawks are shy birds and are rarely seen. But in the southern parts of their range, they have a reputation for being bold and tame.

COMMON BUZZARD *(BUTEO BUTEO)*

True to its name, the common buzzard is one of the most common hawks in its range, particularly in Europe. The common buzzard usually lives in habitats that have at least some trees, but the bird is often seen soaring in the sky. Common buzzards are reddish brown with some white markings scattered throughout their feathers. They have short, broad wings and a short, square-tipped tail.

HOW TO SPOT

Size: 15 to 20 inches (38 to 51 cm) long; 1 to 3 pounds (0.5 to 1.4 kg)

Range: Africa, Asia, and Europe

Habitat: Forests, meadows, moors, and wetlands

Diet: Small mammals

COOPER'S HAWK *(ACCIPITER COOPERII)*

Cooper's hawks are among the most common raptors in North America. They tend to live among people in wooded urban and suburban areas. A Cooper's hawk is about the size of a crow and has long, yellow legs and feet. These birds have bluish-gray heads, wings, and backs. Their chests have dappled white-and-rust–colored patterns. The wings are short and rounded. When they are ready to mate, males pick out a site for the nest and females take the lead in constructing it. These birds are very territorial and will attack any intruders near their nests.

HOW TO SPOT

Size: 13.8 to 19.6 inches (35 to 50 cm) long; 0.6 to 1.2 pounds (0.27 to 0.5 kg)

Range: North America

Habitat: Forests and suburban and urban parks and woodlands

Diet: Small birds, reptiles, amphibians, and small mammals

FUN FACT

Most birds of prey have excellent eyesight to help them hunt. In addition, hawks have ridges above their eyes that offer shade from the sun. This allows them to hunt more efficiently in the daytime.

EURASIAN MARSH HARRIER
(CIRCUS AERUGINOSUS)

The Eurasian marsh harrier is the largest of all harrier species. It has broad wings and a long tail. As the name suggests, these birds live mainly in marshes, but they can also be found in other wetland-type habitats such as rice paddies. Male marsh harriers are usually brown with reddish-brown chests and bellies. Females are larger and have darker-brown, nearly black, feathers.

Male

HOW TO SPOT

Size: 17 to 21 inches (43 to 53 cm) long; 0.9 to 2 pounds (0.4 to 0.9 kg)

Range: Africa, Asia, and Europe

Habitat: Wetlands

Diet: Small aquatic birds, eggs, small mammals, and fish

EURASIAN SPARROWHAWK
(ACCIPITER NISUS)

The Eurasian sparrowhawk is a raptor whose compact size makes it well adapted for hunting in dense tree cover and confined areas. These birds are often seen in suburban and urban environments, where they hunt smaller birds. Male and female sparrowhawks look quite different from one another. Males have bluish-gray backs and wings and orange-and-white stripes on their chests. Females are larger with brown backs and wings and brown-and-white stripes on their chests.

HOW TO SPOT

Size: 11 to 15 inches (28 to 38 cm) long; 0.25 to 0.75 pounds (0.11 to 0.34 kg)

Range: Asia, Europe, and northern Africa

Habitat: Woodlands, farm fields, and suburban and urban gardens

Diet: Small birds and bats

Male

FUN FACT
Eurasian sparrowhawks usually hunt small birds such as sparrows or finches, but they can also capture larger birds such as pigeons.

Female

FERRUGINOUS HAWK
(BUTEO REGALIS)

Ferruginous hawks are the largest hawks in North America. They live in open country such as grasslands but like to nest in cliffs or in the tops of tall trees. Their shoulders and backs have rust-colored feathers. Their undersides are white and spotted with reddish-brown coloring. Ferruginous hawks have long, broad wings with gray tips and gray, white, and rust-colored tails. Females are larger than males.

HOW TO SPOT

Size: 22 to 27 inches (56 to 69 cm) long; 2.2 to 4.4 pounds (1 to 2 kg)

Range: North America

Habitat: Grasslands, plains, valleys, agricultural lands, and the edges of deserts

Diet: Rabbits, ground squirrels, and prairie dogs

FUN FACT
The Latin name for the ferruginous hawk is *Buteo regalis. Buteo* means "hawk." *Regalis* means "kingly." This name was given to the species because of its large and majestic appearance.

HEN HARRIER *(CIRCUS CYANEUS)*

The hen harrier is a raptor that prefers open country in the northern hemisphere, such as in Alaska, Canada, and Europe. Adult male hen harriers are pale gray with white chests and darker markings on their tail feathers. Female hen harriers are brown with striped tail feathers. Hen harriers fly slowly and low over the ground while hunting. These birds also hop and walk across the ground. They do this when picking up prey, looking for materials to make their nests, and grabbing any of their offspring that have wandered too far away.

HOW TO SPOT

Size: 16 to 19.6 inches (41 to 50 cm) long; 0.6 to 1.3 pounds (0.3 to 0.6 kg)

Range: Northern hemisphere

Habitat: Savannas, fields, meadows, prairies, and marshes

Diet: Rodents, birds, and rabbits

Male

Female

NORTHERN GOSHAWK
(ACCIPITER GENTILIS)

Northern goshawks are found throughout the northern hemisphere but are not often seen because of their secretive nature and dense forest habitats. These raptors prefer to hunt by waiting on branches and then diving down onto prey. Northern goshawks have dark-gray backs and wings. The chests, legs, and tail feathers of adults have distinctive gray-and-white stripes.

HOW TO SPOT

Size: 21 to 24 inches (53 to 61 cm) long; 1.3 to 3 pounds (0.6 to 1.4 kg)

Range: Asia, Europe, and North America

Habitat: Forests

Diet: Small mammals and birds

FUN FACT

When a female northern goshawk wants to court a male, she becomes very vocal. In addition, she sometimes takes off into the air and conducts dramatic airborne displays to draw in a mate.

NORTHERN HARRIER
(CIRCUS HUDSONIUS)

Like other harriers, the northern harrier prefers open areas where it can hunt for prey by flying low over the ground. It often nests on the ground too, hiding its chicks in the tall, dense grasses of wetlands. The male northern harrier has a gray head, body, and wings. Its white underside has brown markings. The female northern harrier is mostly brown with a white-and-brown underside. She also has a distinct white ring around her face.

Male

FUN FACT
The northern harrier has a facial disc that is used to help the harrier hear its prey.

Female

HOW TO SPOT

Size: 18 to 20 inches (46 to 51 cm) long; 0.7 to 1.6 pounds (0.3 to 0.7 kg)

Range: North America, Central America, and northern South America

Habitat: Open wetlands, farm fields, grasslands, and coastal sand dunes

Diet: Rodents, birds, frogs, and reptiles

RED-TAILED HAWK
(BUTEO JAMAICENSIS)

The red-tailed hawk is a common sight throughout its expansive range. It can live in a variety of habitats, including deserts, forests, and city parks. Red-tailed hawks build nests made from sticks. They have their nests in high places such as trees, cliffs, and even billboards. Red-tailed hawks can vary greatly in color, but these birds often have mottled-brown bodies, white heads with reddish-brown streaks, and bright, rust-colored tails.

HOW TO SPOT

Size: 18 to 26 inches (46 to 66 cm) long; 1.5 to 3.3 pounds (0.7 to 1.5 kg)

Range: North America and Central America

Habitat: Deserts, grasslands, forests, farm fields, and suburban and urban areas

Diet: Small mammals, birds, reptiles, and carrion

ROUGH-LEGGED HAWK
(BUTEO LAGOPUS)

The rough-legged hawk is an Arctic bird. It spends much of the year in the far northern parts of the northern hemisphere, where it lives and nests in the tundra. When it migrates south in the winter, the rough-legged hawk prefers open areas, such as grasslands, that look like its northern home. The rough-legged hawk is known for its diversity of color patterns and markings. Some of these hawks can be completely black, gray, or white. Others have mottled-brown and striped feathers.

FUN FACT
The rough-legged hawk gets its name from its feather-covered legs, which help keep the bird warm.

HOW TO SPOT

Size: 19 to 20 inches (48 to 51 cm) long; 1.5 to 3 pounds (0.7 to 1.4 kg)
Range: Northern parts of Asia, Europe, and North America
Habitat: Tundra, subarctic forests, wetlands, and grasslands
Diet: Lemmings, voles, other small mammals, and birds

RUFOUS CRAB HAWK
(BUTEOGALLUS AEQUINOCTIALIS)

Many hawks eat a variety of prey, but the rufous crab hawk eats only crabs. It usually dives down onto the crab and takes it back to its perch to eat. Rufous crab hawks live along the coast of northeastern South America. The bird has a dark-brown back and head and a reddish-brown underside with thin, brown stripes. Its feet and the base of its beak—called the cere—are yellow or orange.

HOW TO SPOT

Size: 16.5 to 18 inches (42 to 46 cm) long; 1 to 2 pounds (0.5 to 0.9 kg)
Range: Northeastern South America
Habitat: Coastal areas, mangroves, and river edges
Diet: Crabs

THE TERM RUFOUS

Many birds, such as the rufous crab hawk, have the word *rufous* in their names. *Rufous* means "reddish" and refers to the bird's primary color.

SHARP-SHINNED HAWK
(ACCIPITER STRIATUS)

The sharp-shinned hawk is an incredibly agile flyer. Its small size and short wings help it quickly navigate forests and dense vegetation. This hawk can even catch its prey while flying and will then pluck its prey prior to consuming it. The sharp-shinned hawk doesn't need to drink water. The hawk gets all the water it needs from its food. The wings, back, and crown of a sharp-shinned hawk are grayish brown, and its underside is white with reddish-brown stripes. In flight, white-and-brown stripes are clearly seen on its wings and square-tipped tail.

HOW TO SPOT

Size: 9.4 to 13.4 inches (24 to 34 cm) long; 0.4 to 1.1 pounds (0.19 to 0.5 kg)

Range: North America, Central America, and South America

Habitat: Forests

Diet: Birds

FUN FACT

The sharp-shinned hawk is known by several common names, including sharpie, blue darter, little blue darter, and bird hawk.

SWAMP HARRIER
(CIRCUS APPROXIMANS)

The swamp harrier gets its common name from where it lives: in wetlands such as swamps, marshes, and coastal areas. This medium-sized raptor feeds on nearly any small animal in its habitat, including insects, birds, and fish. It hunts by flying low over the ground and sometimes wades in shallow water to find prey. Swamp harriers are mottled brown and white with visible white rumps, but sometimes they appear to have completely brown bodies.

FUN FACT

Because they live in habitats without many trees, swamp harriers build their platform nests on the ground among tall reeds or grasses.

HOW TO SPOT

Size: 18 to 24 inches (46 to 61 cm) long; 1.3 to 2.4 pounds (0.6 to 1 kg)

Range: New Zealand, Australia, and the Pacific islands

Habitat: Coastal wetlands, freshwater wetlands, grasslands, and farm fields

Diet: Small mammals, birds, eggs, reptiles, fish, insects, and carrion

ZONE-TAILED HAWK
(BUTEO ALBONOTATUS)

The zone-tailed hawk is a grayish-black bird that can be recognized by the wide, white band marking its long tail. This hawk builds its large, bowl-like nests in the tops of deciduous trees such as willows and cottonwoods. Because they share the same habitat, range, and color patterns, zone-tailed hawks are often mistaken for common black hawks.

HOW TO SPOT

Size: 17 to 22 inches (43 to 56 cm) long; 1.4 to 1.8 pounds (0.6 to 0.8 kg)

Range: North America, Central America, and South America

Habitat: Forests and desert uplands

Diet: Small birds, amphibians, reptiles, and rodents

BLACK KITE *(MILVUS MIGRANS)*

Black kites are highly adaptable birds. They have a diverse diet and can live in many different habitats, from semidesert areas to coasts. They're known for living in human-populated areas, sometimes scavenging for food at garbage dumps or stealing food from outdoor markets. Despite its name, the black kite is mostly reddish brown. It has a squared-off tail and a hooked beak that's black at the tip.

HOW TO SPOT

Size: 17 to 25 inches (43 to 64 cm) long; 1.4 to 2.4 pounds (0.6 to 1.1 kg)

Range: Africa, Asia, Australia, and Europe

Habitat: Grasslands, wetlands, open areas near lakes, semidesert areas, and coasts

Diet: Carrion, small mammals, amphibians, reptiles, fish, and insects

WHAT ARE KITES?

Kites are small raptors that belong to three different subfamilies. While they can look quite different from one another, some common physical characteristics they share include short beaks, small heads, and long, narrow wings and tails.

EUROPEAN HONEY BUZZARD
(PERNIS APIVORUS)

European honey buzzards live in forests, where they search out their favorite foods: wasps and hornets. When a honey buzzard finds a wasp or hornet nest, it knocks the nest to the ground. Then the bird digs out the larvae and adult insects with its claws to eat them. Honey buzzards are large birds with broad wings and long tails. They're usually mottled brown and white, but their color pattern can vary greatly between individual birds.

FUN FACT
Since honey buzzards eat wasp and hornet larvae and adult insects, chunks of wax comb from the insects' nests are often found near honey buzzard nests.

HOW TO SPOT

Size: 20 to 23 inches (51 to 58 cm) long; 0.9 to 2.3 pounds (0.4 to 1.0 kg)

Range: Africa, Asia, and Europe

Habitat: Forests

Diet: Wasps and hornets (larvae and adults), other insects, and small mammals

41

HOOK-BILLED KITE
(CHONDROHIERAX UNCINATUS)

The hook-billed kite is a tropical bird that feeds mainly on tree snails in the rain forest canopy. The bird uses its large, hooked beak to break open larger snail shells but will also swallow small snails whole. Hook-billed kites usually have gray heads and gray or brown backs. Their chests and the undersides of their tails and wings have gray-and-white or brown-and-white stripes. They also have colorful patches of green and yellow near their eyes.

HOW TO SPOT

Size: 15 to 20 inches (38 to 51 cm) long; 0.4 to 0.8 pounds (0.2 to 0.36 kg)

Range: Central America and South America

Habitat: Rain forests and scrublands

Diet: Tree snails, reptiles, amphibians, crabs, and insects

LETTER-WINGED KITE
(ELANUS SCRIPTUS)

Letter-winged kites are not often seen. Not only are they rare, they're also mainly nocturnal and spend their nights hunting rodents, especially rats. These small, gray-and-white raptors have bold, black patches on top of and underneath their wings. They also have black markings around their striking red eyes.

FUN FACT

While most raptors are quiet, letter-winged kites have a reputation for being noisy and will whistle, call, and chatter.

HOW TO SPOT

Size: 13 to 14 inches (33 to 36 cm) long; 0.35 to 0.9 pounds (0.16 to 0.4 kg)

Range: Australia

Habitat: Grasslands and dry woodlands

Diet: Rodents

MISSISSIPPI KITE
(ICTINIA MISSISSIPPIENSIS)

Mississippi kites are social birds that often nest and flock in large groups. The Mississippi kite is about the size of a crow and is an acrobatic flyer that can catch insects in flight. Its head, chest, and underwings are light gray, and the top of its wings are darker gray. It also has distinctive gray marks around its eyes.

HOW TO SPOT

Size: 13 to 15 inches (33 to 38 cm) long; 0.5 to 0.9 pounds (0.2 to 0.4 kg)

Range: North America, Central America, and South America

Habitat: Forests, shortgrass prairies, and urban and suburban areas

Diet: Insects, small mammals, lizards, and reptiles

FUN FACT
Mississippi kites will hunt both alone and in groups. They've been seen hunting in large flocks of more than 25 birds.

PEARL KITE *(GAMPSONYX SWAINSONII)*

The pearl kite is small and sleek. It has mottled-gray wings and is mostly white on its underside. It can also be identified by the black markings on its head that look like a cap and mask. Pearl kites often eat small lizards. They dive down on their prey from perches on high shrubs or trees.

HOW TO SPOT

Size: 7 to 11 inches (18 to 28 cm) long; 0.2 to 0.25 pounds (0.09 to 0.11 kg)

Range: Central America and South America

Habitat: Dry pastures, savannas, and open tropical forests

Diet: Small lizards and large insects

SNAIL KITE *(ROSTRHAMUS SOCIABILIS)*

Snail kites have very limited diets. They eat freshwater snails, specifically the apple snail. That's why snail kites make their homes in and around freshwater habitats such as marshes and shallow lakes. In the United States, snail kites are found only in Florida. They also have wider ranges in Central and South America. These birds are mainly dark gray and have bright-orange feet and orange-and-gray hooked beaks.

HOW TO SPOT

Size: 14 to 16 inches (36 to 41 cm) long; 0.88 to 1.3 pounds (0.4 to 0.6 kg)

Range: Southern North America, Central America, and South America

Habitat: Wetlands

Diet: Freshwater snails

FUN FACT

The snail kite was once called the everglade kite because scientists first recorded its presence in the Florida Everglades in 1844.

SQUARE-TAILED KITE
(LOPHOICTINIA ISURA)

The square-tailed kite is found only in Australia. It commonly nests in open forests or other habitats with tree cover. It is a slender bird with long wings that fan out into individual feathers that look like fingers. It has a square-shaped tail. The square-tailed kite has a reddish-brown chest, dark-brown wings, and a white or pale-tan face.

HOW TO SPOT

Size: 19 to 22 inches (48 to 56 cm) long; 1 to 1.5 pounds (0.5 to 0.7 kg)

Range: Australia

Habitat: Open forests

Diet: Small birds, eggs, insects, reptiles, and tree frogs

SWALLOW-TAILED KITE
(ELANOIDES FORFICATUS)

The swallow-tailed kite is a small, graceful bird. It is recognizable by its deeply forked tail and bold black-and-white coloring. Its head and underside are bright white. The bird's wings, back, and long tail are dark gray to black. Swallow-tailed kites prefer to live in areas with tall trees, where they build their nests.

FUN FACT
Swallow-tailed kites sometimes hunt for prey in small groups.

HOW TO SPOT

Size: 20 to 25 inches (51 to 64 cm) long; 0.8 to 1.3 pounds (0.4 to 0.6 kg)

Range: Southeastern North America, Central America, and South America

Habitat: Wetlands and lowland forests

Diet: Flying insects, frogs, reptiles, and fish

WHISTLING KITE
(HALIASTUR SPHENURUS)

The whistling kite earned its name by being a very vocal bird—its most common call sounds like a whistle. It has a body shape that's like a sea eagle's, which is why it's sometimes called the whistling eagle. Male and female whistling kites are mottled brown with darker-brown wings. When they fly and reveal their undersides, observers can see a few white feathers in the centers of both wings.

HOW TO SPOT

Size: 20 to 23 inches (51 to 58 cm) long; 0.8 to 2.4 pounds (0.4 to 1.1 kg)

Range: Australia and New Guinea

Habitat: Forests, rain forests, and savannas

Diet: Small mammals, birds, reptiles, amphibians, and carrion

BEARDED VULTURE
(GYPAETUS BARBATUS)

Bearded vultures are large birds that are not often seen because they live in high, remote mountains. They build their large nests in caves or on the edges of cliffs. Bearded vultures have gray or black wings and backs. They have rusty-white heads and undersides. True to its name, the bearded vulture also has some black feathers at the base of its beak that look like a beard. The bird has a large wingspan of 7.5 to 9.2 feet (2.3 to 2.8 m).

HOW TO SPOT

Size: 37 to 50 inches (94 to 127 cm) long; 10 to 16 pounds (4.5 to 7.2 kg)

Range: Africa, Asia, and Europe

Habitat: Mountains and plains near mountains

Diet: Bones

FUN FACT
Bones make up 90 percent of a bearded vulture's diet.

EGYPTIAN VULTURE
(NEOPHRON PERCNOPTERUS)

Since they prefer to eat carrion, Egyptian vultures can often be seen scavenging in landfills or garbage dumps in populated areas. The Egyptian vulture is small for a vulture. It has a color pattern that's mainly white, including white feathered legs. But it has dark markings on its wings and tail. Egyptian vultures also have bare, yellow faces and hooked beaks.

HOW TO SPOT

Size: 21 to 27 inches (53 to 69 cm) long; 3.5 to 5 pounds (1.6 to 2.3 kg)

Range: Africa, Asia, and Europe

Habitat: Deserts, steppes, and dry pastures

Diet: Carrion and some small mammals

WHAT ARE OLD WORLD VULTURES?

There are 15 species of Old World vultures. These vultures eat carrion and have special adaptations that help them do this. They have excellent eyesight for spotting carrion, strong feet and beaks for grasping fur and flesh, and bald heads that are easier to keep clean than if they were feathered.

EURASIAN GRIFFON *(GYPS FULVUS)*

During nesting season, Eurasian griffons live along high cliffs or caves in colonies. For the rest of the year, they prefer dry habitats such as steppes, where they can scavenge for carrion, their main food source. Eurasian griffons have long necks and heads that are mainly white. Their bodies are pale brown, and they have darker feathers on their wings. They are the most common vulture throughout their range.

HOW TO SPOT

Size: 36 to 43 inches (91 to 109 cm) long; 13 to 24 pounds (6 to 11 kg)

Range: Africa, Asia, and Europe

Habitat: Mountains, plateaus, steppes, and semidesert areas

Diet: Carrion

HIMALAYAN GRIFFON
(GYPS HIMALAYENSIS)

The Himalayan griffon is a large vulture that's found throughout the Himalayan Mountains and surrounding areas. Although they're usually alone or in pairs, Himalayan griffons will often gather in large groups around a carcass to feed and squabble with one another. The Himalayan griffon has a large, pale-brown body; dark markings on its wings; and a pale, featherless head.

FUN FACT

Himalayan griffons live at high elevations among some of the tallest mountains on Earth. They've been recorded at elevations as high as 19,600 feet (6,000 m).

HOW TO SPOT

Size: 40 to 43 inches (102 to 109 cm) long; 17 to 26 pounds (7.7 to 12 kg)

Range: Asia

Habitat: Mountains

Diet: Carrion

HOODED VULTURE
(NECROSYRTES MONACHUS)

The hooded vulture is a critically endangered species that lives in open areas in Africa. The bird has a dark-brown body. Its pink face is featherless, but there is a velvety layer of short, whitish feathers on the top and back of its head. Hooded vultures can also be recognized by the blue rings around their eyes.

HOW TO SPOT

Size: 21 to 22 inches (53 to 56 cm) long; 3 to 6 pounds (1.4 to 2.7 kg)
Range: Africa
Habitat: Open forests and savannas
Diet: Carrion and small insects

FUN FACT
Hooded vultures are often the first to spot carrion. However, when larger and more aggressive vulture species arrive, they must wait to eat whatever is left.

INDIAN VULTURE *(GYPS INDICUS)*

Indian vultures live in the eastern half of India. They soar over open plains and use their excellent eyesight to spot animal carcasses on the ground. These birds can also be found living in agricultural areas or in parks in villages or cities. The Indian vulture is a large, bulky bird with a light-brown body. It has a thin layer of whitish down feathers along its long neck and head.

HOW TO SPOT

Size: 32 to 35 inches (81 to 89 cm) long; 12 to 14 pounds (5.4 to 6.4 kg)

Range: India

Habitat: Plains and agricultural or urban areas

Diet: Carrion

RED-HEADED VULTURE
(SARCOGYPS CALVUS)

Red-headed vultures have striking coloring that makes them easy to distinguish from other vulture species. Their bodies are covered in black feathers and their nearly bald heads and feet are reddish orange. The ends of their hooked beaks are black. Red-headed vultures are increasingly endangered throughout their range in India and Southeast Asia. This is largely because the livestock carcasses they feed on were treated with a drug that's harmful to the vultures.

HOW TO SPOT

Size: 30 to 33 inches (76 to 84 cm) long; 8 to 12 pounds (3.6 to 5.4 kg)

Range: India and Southeast Asia

Habitat: Savannas, forests, and agricultural areas

Diet: Carrion

RÜPPELL'S GRIFFON
(GYPS RUEPPELLI)

Due to its uniquely patterned feathers, the Rüppell's griffon appears to have scales along its back and wings. The feathers covering the upper part of its body are grayish brown with pale tips. Rüppell's griffons have pale-gray heads, hooked beaks, and necks that are covered with a thin layer of down. Although they scavenge in open areas, these birds prefer to nest in colonies on high cliffs.

FUN FACT
Rüppell's griffons are the world's highest-flying birds. They can soar as high as 36,000 feet (10,900 m) above sea level.

HOW TO SPOT

Size: 40 inches (102 cm) long; 15 to 20 pounds (6.8 to 9.1 kg)
Range: Africa
Habitat: Steppes, arid grasslands, and mountains
Diet: Carrion

ANDEAN CONDOR *(VULTUR GRYPHUS)*

The Andean condor's massive size means that it needs some help getting into the air. That's one of the reasons it lives in high mountains. The winds and air currents at these high altitudes help this bird lift off the ground. Both male and female Andean condors have bald heads. Their bodies are covered in black feathers, and they have fluffy, white feathers that look like collars around their necks. Male Andean condors have a large comb above their beaks—much like a rooster's.

Male

HOW TO SPOT

Size: 40 to 51 inches (102 to 130 cm) long; 17 to 33 pounds (7.7 to 15 kg)

Range: Andes Mountains in South America

Habitat: Mountains and coastal desert plains

Diet: Carrion

FUN FACT

At up to 10.5 feet (3.2 m) wide, the Andean condor has the longest wingspan of any raptor.

NEW AND OLD WORLD VULTURES

Although the seven species of New World vultures share the common name *vulture* and can look similar to Old World vultures, the two groups are not closely related. Condors are a type of New World vulture. Like Old World vultures, the condors are large birds with bald heads and strong beaks. Their feet, however, are flat and relatively weak, and condors usually live in warmer climates compared to Old World vultures.

BLACK VULTURE (*CORAGYPS ATRATUS*)

Black vultures can be seen foraging along roadsides, where they feed on roadkill. They prefer to forage in open areas, but black vultures are also found roosting in tall trees in large groups. Black vultures are covered in black feathers. Their bald heads and feet are grayish black. When they fly, silvery-white patches are visible on the undersides of their wings. Black vultures are aggressive and will scare away other vultures around carcasses. They will sometimes grunt, hiss, or let out low barks when squabbling over food.

HOW TO SPOT

Size: 24 to 27 inches (60 to 68 cm) long; 3.5 to 5 pounds (1.6 to 2.3 kg)

Range: North America, Central America, and South America

Habitat: Lowlands, deserts, open fields, and urban and rural areas

Diet: Carrion

CALIFORNIA CONDOR
(GYMNOGYPS CALIFORNIANUS)

The California condor is a critically endangered bird. It is found only in desert areas in California and a few neighboring states. It's the largest flying bird in North America. Like other vultures, the California condor eats carrion. Its body is covered in shaggy, black feathers. It has a bald head and neck that range from yellow to orange. The California condor can soar in the air for an hour without flapping its wings. It has been known to fly more than 100 miles (160 km) in a single day as it looks for food, but it always comes back to its nest.

HOW TO SPOT

Size: 42 to 54 inches (107 to 137 cm) long; 18 to 31 pounds (8.2 to 14 kg)

Range: Southwestern North America

Habitat: Deserts

Diet: Carrion

SAVING THE CONDOR

In 1967, the California condor was put on the endangered species list. By 1987, there were only 27 of these birds left in the wild. The species was close to extinction. Conservationists started a captive breeding program, releasing more condors into the wild. By 2021, the California condor population was at approximately 440 birds.

TURKEY VULTURE *(CATHARTES AURA)*

Turkey vultures are the most widespread vultures in their range, living throughout the Americas. The turkey vulture's large body is covered in black feathers. It has a small, featherless red head and pink legs. The turkey vulture's incredible sense of smell means that it often finds carrion before other vultures. Turkey vultures often target small carcasses. That way, they can finish their meals before other vulture species arrive.

FUN FACT

Turkey vultures ward off threats with an unusual form of self-defense—they vomit stomach acid onto whatever is frightening them.

HOW TO SPOT

Size: 25 to 32 inches (64 to 81 cm) long; 4.5 pounds (2 kg)

Range: North America, Central America, and South America

Habitat: Farmlands, forests, and hilly areas

Diet: Carrion

CHIMANGO CARACARA
(MILVAGO CHIMANGO)

The chimango caracara is a small raptor that flies and scavenges in noisy groups. These birds are common throughout southern South America. They often live alongside humans in towns or cities if there are areas such as parks where they can find prey. The chimango caracara is mostly mottled brown with some darker streaks, and it has bare skin on its face that's reddish pink in females and yellow in males. The feathers on the undersides of its wings are striped.

HOW TO SPOT

Size: 12 to 17 inches (30 to 43 cm) long; 0.4 to 0.7 pounds (0.2 to 0.3 kg)
Range: South America
Habitat: Wetlands, fields, open forests, parks, and foothills
Diet: Carrion, insects, eggs, and small mammals

Female

WHAT ARE CARACARAS?

Caracaras are a subfamily of bird species within the falcon family. There are ten species of caracaras, and they live only in the Americas, usually in warm climates. Caracaras can be recognized by their long legs and areas of bare skin on their faces.

CRESTED CARACARA
(CARACARA PLANCUS)

The crested caracara is easily recognized by its bold, black-and-white coloring and the black crest on its head. It also has a bare yellow-orange face and hooked gray bill. This bird has a reputation for eating carrion because it's often spotted alongside roads. However, the crested caracara has a very diverse diet. It will eat almost anything, including other birds and their eggs, and even snakes.

FUN FACT
Using their long legs and tails for balance, crested caracaras often walk along the ground as they search for prey.

HOW TO SPOT

Size: 19 to 23 inches (48 to 58 cm) long; 2.5 to 2.75 pounds (1.1 to 1.25 kg)

Range: North America, Central America, and South America

Habitat: Deserts, grasslands, and farm fields

Diet: Carrion, mammals, birds, eggs, reptiles, and insects

RED-THROATED CARACARA
(IBYCTER AMERICANUS)

Red-throated caracaras are known for being noisy, social birds, yet they prefer to hunt alone. They fly through the forest canopy looking for insects, especially nests of paper wasps. They've also been known to eat fruits. The red-throated caracara has a black body, a white belly, and a red, featherless face. Its beak is gray at the base and yellow at the tip.

FUN FACT
Red-throated caracaras seem to be immune to wasp stings, and wasps flee their nests when caracaras attack, leaving the larvae behind.

HOW TO SPOT

Size: 21 to 25 inches (53 to 64 cm) long; 1.1 to 1.3 pounds (0.5 to 0.6 kg)

Range: Central America and South America

Habitat: Lowland evergreen forests

Diet: Insects, larvae, lizards, and fruits

YELLOW-HEADED CARACARA
(MILVAGO CHIMACHIMA)

The yellow-headed caracara is a cream-colored bird with dark-brown wings and a single black stripe behind each eye. Yellow-headed caracaras have areas of bare skin on their faces that are pale pink in females and orange in males. These caracaras are common throughout their range and can live in a variety of open habitats such as wetlands or farmlands. They have a varied diet. They will eat carrion and live prey such as grasshoppers or lizards.

Male

HOW TO SPOT

Size: 15 to 17 inches (38 to 43 cm) long; 0.5 to 0.7 pounds (0.2 to 0.3 kg)

Range: Central America and South America

Habitat: Fields, wetlands, palm savannas, and agricultural areas

Diet: Carrion, amphibians, reptiles, insects, and fruits

Female

APLOMADO FALCON
(FALCO FEMORALIS)

Like other falcons, aplomado falcons are fast and acrobatic flyers. They can catch prey such as insects and birds in the air. This small raptor has a gray body, a black-and-white–patterned head, and a rusty-orange belly. Aplomado falcons also have long tails and legs.

HOW TO SPOT

Size: 15 to 17 inches (38 to 43 cm) long; 0.4 to 0.9 pounds (0.17 to 0.4 kg)

Range: North America, Central America, and South America

Habitat: Coastal prairies and desert grasslands

Diet: Birds, insects, rodents, and lizards

FUN FACT

The aplomado falcon gets its name from its gray markings. The Spanish word *aplomado* means "lead colored" or "gray."

BAT FALCON *(FALCO RUFIGULARIS)*

Bat falcons hunt along forest edges at dawn or dusk because their main food source is nocturnal: bats. But along with bats, bat falcons also eat other birds and large insects such as grasshoppers or dragonflies. The bat falcon is a small, compact bird. It is dark brown or black with a collar of white feathers. Its belly and legs are rusty orange. The bat falcon has a long tail that's black and streaked with thin, gray or white markings. This bird also has a small, sharp beak that helps it easily rip into prey.

HOW TO SPOT

Size: 7 to 12 inches (18 to 30 cm) long; 0.25 to 0.5 pounds (0.1 to 0.2 kg)

Range: Mexico, Central America, and South America

Habitat: Tropical forests

Diet: Bats, birds, and large insects

FALCONIDAE FAMILY

The Falconidae family contains nearly 60 species, including falcons, caracaras, and falconets. The birds in this family are known for being fast and powerful fliers. Their long, pointed wings allow them to fly and dive rapidly. Most Falconidae species have notched beaks that help them kill their prey.

EURASIAN HOBBY *(FALCO SUBBUTEO)*

Eurasian hobbies are small and sleek falcons with long, pointed wings that help them perform incredible aerial maneuvers. They specialize in hunting flying insects and birds, so they usually live in habitats such as forests and wetlands where these animals are found. The Eurasian hobby has a dark grayish-brown body and head and a rust-colored patch on its lower belly. The undersides of its wings and its chest are dappled brown and white.

FUN FACT

The Eurasian hobby is such a fast and skilled flyer that it catches and eats most of its prey in the air.

HOW TO SPOT

Size: 11 to 14 inches (28 to 36 cm) long; 0.3 to 0.75 pounds (0.1 to 0.34 kg)

Range: Africa, Asia, and Europe

Habitat: Open forests, fields, and wetlands

Diet: Flying insects and small birds

GRAY FALCON *(FALCO HYPOLEUCOS)*

Gray falcons are stocky birds that are mostly gray. They have dark-gray wings and backs. Their chests and heads are pale gray. Their beaks and feet are yellow, and they have yellow rings around their eyes. The gray falcon's main diet is other birds, and it will even hunt large birds that are similar to it in size, such as parrots or pigeons. These falcons will stay in old nests made by other birds, preferably ones that are high up and close to water.

HOW TO SPOT

Size: 13 to 17 inches (33 to 43 cm) long; 0.75 to 1.4 pounds (0.34 to 0.6 kg)
Range: Australia
Habitat: Forests, savannas, dunes, and plains
Diet: Birds, small mammals, and insects

GYRFALCON *(FALCO RUSTICOLUS)*

The gyrfalcon is the largest of all falcon species. It is so large as an adult that it has no natural predators in its range. However, injured or young gyrfalcons can become prey to foxes, wolverines, grizzly bears, and even great horned owls. The gyrfalcon is not often seen because of its remote habitat in the far northern hemisphere. This bird can vary in color, from all-white to all-brown and many variations in between. Gyrfalcons primarily hunt other large birds, especially the ptarmigan—an Artic bird species. Gyrfalcons often reuse the stick nests of other bird species.

HOW TO SPOT

Size: 19 to 25 inches (48 to 64 cm) long; 1.5 to 4.75 pounds (0.7 to 2.15 kg)

Range: Circumpolar, including parts of Asia, Europe, and North America

Habitat: Arctic and alpine tundra

Diet: Large birds and small mammals

LAUGHING FALCON
(HERPETOTHERES CACHINNANS)

The laughing falcon's common name comes from the yelping sounds the bird makes in the morning and at night. This forest bird is easy to recognize by its bold, black-and-white pattern. Its head is white with a black mask, and its body is white or cream, contrasting with its black wings. The underside of its tail has black-and-white stripes. Small snakes are a laughing falcon's favorite meal. It will swoop down on a snake, grasp it behind the head, and sometimes rip the head off before eating it.

HOW TO SPOT

Size: 17 to 22 inches (43 to 56 cm) long; 0.9 to 1.7 pounds (0.4 to 0.8 kg)

Range: Central and South America

Habitat: Open forests and savannas

Diet: Snakes, rodents, and fish

FUN FACT
The laughing falcon will eat venomous snake species such as coral snakes and rattlesnakes.

MERLIN *(FALCO COLUMBARIUS)*

Merlins are small falcons that live in both rural and urban areas within their range. This fast and adaptable bird sometimes hunts from perches and sometimes by flying low, undetected, over the ground as it searches for prey. While male and female merlins have similar patterns—solid-colored wings, streaked undersides, and striped tails—they differ in color. A male's upperparts are either slaty blue, dark brown, or purplish. He has black coloring from his head and down to his shoulders and back. Females are different shades of brown with yellow-banded tails.

HOW TO SPOT

Size: 10 to 12 inches (25 to 30 cm) long; 0.3 to 0.4 pounds (0.1 to 0.2 kg)

Range: Africa, Asia, Europe, and North America

Habitat: Forests, prairies, and urban and rural areas

Diet: Birds, insects, small mammals, and reptiles

Male

FUN FACT

After mating, a female merlin stays at the nest to care for the eggs. The male hunts for food but doesn't approach the female when she's in the nest. Instead, he leaves food nearby for her to grab.

Female

PEREGRINE FALCON
(FALCO PEREGRINUS)

Peregrine falcons are the fastest birds in the world. When diving, they can reach speeds of up to 200 miles per hour (320 kmh). Peregrine falcons also have an impressive range. They're found on every continent except Antarctica and live in a variety of habitats. These medium-sized raptors have bluish-gray wings, backs, and heads with rings of yellow around their eyes. Their bellies and the undersides of their wings have black-and-white stripes.

HOW TO SPOT

Size: 14 to 22 inches (36 to 56 cm) long; 1.4 to 2 pounds (0.6 to 0.9 kg)

Range: Africa, Asia, Australia, Europe, North America, Central America, and South America

Habitat: Variable, including seacoasts, mountains, wetlands, urban areas, and open valleys

Diet: Birds and small mammals

A WANDERING BIRD

Peregrine means "wanderer," which is how the peregrine falcon got its name. This bird appears nearly everywhere in the world and has a reputation for being a long-distance traveler. Some peregrines migrate up to 15,000 miles (24,100 km).

PRAIRIE FALCON *(FALCO MEXICANUS)*

Prairie falcons are found only in the dry, western regions of North America. Their feathers help them blend into the surrounding brown landscape. Their backs and wings are mottled brown while their chests are white with brown spots. The prairie falcon has a distinctive dark band across its face that looks like a mustache. This medium-sized raptor hunts by flying low to the ground and surprising its prey.

HOW TO SPOT

Size: 14 to 18 inches (36 to 46 cm) long; 0.9 to 2.2 pounds (0.4 to 1 kg)

Range: North America

Habitat: Prairies with cliffs or bluffs

Diet: Ground squirrels and birds

PYGMY FALCON
(POLIHIERAX SEMITORQUATUS)

The pygmy falcon is the smallest raptor in Africa. These small birds hunt prey—usually lizards such as skinks or large insects—by pouncing on the creatures from above. Both male and female pygmy falcons have gray wings and a gray cap on their heads. In addition, females have a large patch of brown on their backs.

HOW TO SPOT

Size: 7 to 8 inches (18 to 20 cm) long; 0.09 to 0.12 pounds (0.04 to 0.085 kg)
Range: Africa
Habitat: Scrublands, savannas, and steppes
Diet: Small lizards and small insects

Male, *left*, and female, *right*

FUN FACT
Pygmy falcons don't build their own nests. Instead, they use nesting chambers in communal nests made by weaver birds.

SAKER FALCON *(FALCO CHERRUG)*

The saker falcon is the second-largest falcon species in the world. Most of the time, saker falcons hunt their prey by flying horizontally, not by diving. Saker falcons can vary in patterns and colors. They may have a chocolate-brown color, or they could be cream colored with brown streaks and bars. The saker falcon is quite aggressive and relentless. It doesn't easily give up on prey once it has it in its sight. This quality makes saker falcons prized by falconers, who train the birds and use them to hunt.

HOW TO SPOT

Size: 17 to 22 inches (43 to 56 cm) long; 1.5 to 3 pounds (0.7 to 1.4 kg)
Range: Africa, Asia, and Europe
Habitat: Grasslands, steppes, and open woodlands
Diet: Small mammals

TAITA FALCON *(FALCO FASCIINUCHA)*

The Taita falcon is a small, rare species that lives only in a few areas in Africa. Although in flight it can be mistaken for a peregrine falcon, the Taita falcon has a shorter tail and reddish-brown feathers on its underside. The Taita falcon also has a dark-gray head and wings and a white patch at its throat. It prefers dry, open habitats with cliffs or tall trees where it can nest.

FUN FACT
The Taita falcon is named for the hills in Kenya where it was first seen.

HOW TO SPOT

Size: 10 to 11 inches (25 to 28 cm) long; 0.4 to 0.75 pounds (0.2 to 0.34 kg)

Range: Africa

Habitat: Dry woodlands, savannas, cliffs, and gorges

Diet: Small birds and large insects

COLLARED FALCONET
(MICROHIERAX CAERULESCENS)

The collared falconet is a tiny falcon with a white face and a black mask around its eyes. The collared falconet's wings are also black. Its throat and belly are rusty orange. Because of its small size, its prey is small too. The collared falconet usually eats insects.

HOW TO SPOT

Size: 5.5 to 7 inches (14 to 18 cm) long; 0.06 to 0.1 pounds (0.03 to 0.05 kg)
Range: Southeast Asia
Habitat: Open forests near rivers and streams
Diet: Insects

WHAT ARE FALCONETS?

Small raptors such as falconets hunt prey like larger raptors do, but the animals they eat are much smaller. Falconets hunt insects and small mammals. The collared falconet eats mainly one type of insect: butterflies.

PIED FALCONET
(MICROHIERAX MELANOLEUCOS)

The pied falconet has black coloring on its back with a white throat and underside. It also has a wide, black mask near its eyes. These birds are often seen in family groups of between four and 20 birds. Pied falconets catch their insect prey in flight after making quick, aggressive attacks.

HOW TO SPOT

Size: 6 to 7.5 inches (15 to 19 cm) long; 0.1 to 0.2 pounds (0.05 to 0.1 kg)

Range: Southeast Asia

Habitat: Open forests near rivers and streams

Diet: Large insects and small bats

FUN FACT
Falconet species are the smallest birds of prey.

AMERICAN KESTREL
(FALCO SPARVERIUS)

American kestrels are the smallest and most common falcons in North America. These agile birds hunt by watching for prey from tall perches or by hovering above the ground. Males have wings and crowns that are blue gray, and females are reddish brown in these areas. Adult American kestrels have either light or no spotting on their breasts. They also have a black-and-white pattern on their faces, along with two noticeable black lines.

FUN FACT
American kestrels take dust baths. They use their wings to kick up dust and spray it on their bodies.

Male

HOW TO SPOT

Size: 8.5 to 12 inches (22 to 30 cm) long; 0.2 to 0.4 pounds (0.1 to 0.2 kg)

Range: North America, Central America, and South America

Habitat: Meadows, grasslands, deserts, and farm fields

Diet: Large insects and small rodents

EURASIAN KESTREL
(FALCO TINNUNCULUS)

Eurasian kestrels hunt in open areas, and they are often seen along roads or even at airports within their range. They search for prey by hovering above the ground where they may spot small mammals to eat. Male Eurasian kestrels have gray heads, spotted and rusty-brown backs, and gray tails with black tips. Females are rusty brown with a black, spotted pattern on their heads, backs, and tails. Both males and females have dark markings under their eyes.

Male

HOW TO SPOT

Size: 12.5 to 13.5 inches (32 to 34 cm) long; 0.3 to 0.6 pounds (0.1 to 0.3 kg)
Range: Africa, Asia, and Europe
Habitat: Grasslands, moorlands, farm fields, and suburban and urban areas
Diet: Small birds, small mammals, and insects

Female

FUN FACT
Eurasian kestrels are known by many names, including the common kestrel and European kestrel.

GRAY KESTREL *(FALCO ARDOSIACEUS)*

The gray kestrel is a small raptor that lives in just a few regions on the African continent. Its entire body is covered in gray feathers. The bird has bright yellow around its eyes and at the base of its beak. It also has bright-yellow feet. Gray kestrels live in forests, where they hunt large insects, such as grasshoppers, or small rodents and birds.

HOW TO SPOT

Size: 11 to 13 inches (28 to 33 cm) long; 0.4 to 0.6 pounds (0.2 to 0.3 kg)

Range: Africa

Habitat: Forests and wet savannas

Diet: Large insects, small rodents, and small birds

GREATER KESTREL
(FALCO RUPICOLOIDES)

The greater kestrel doesn't weigh much, but it's the largest of all kestrels. These small raptors prefer open areas so they can hunt, but they also need to be near a few trees for roosting and nesting. Greater kestrels are pale brown with black barring or spots. Their gray tails have broad, black stripes.

HOW TO SPOT

Size: 11 to 14.5 inches (28 to 37 cm) long; 0.4 to 0.7 pounds (0.2 to 0.3 kg)

Range: Africa

Habitat: Deserts, steppes, and grasslands

Diet: Insects, small birds, lizards, and small mammals

FUN FACT
A greater kestrel will sometimes hide its food in tufts of grass and come back for it later.

NANKEEN KESTREL
(FALCO CENCHROIDES)

The nankeen kestrel is a small raptor. It is commonly seen throughout Australia and parts of New Guinea. Although nankeen kestrels prefer open forests and fields, they are an adaptable species that can live and nest in a variety of habitats. Nankeen kestrels are mostly reddish brown with darker streaks on top. They are pale tan or white underneath. They have black bands at the ends of their tail feathers.

HOW TO SPOT

Size: 12 to 14 inches (30 to 36 cm) long; 0.25 to 0.6 pounds (0.11 to 0.3 kg)

Range: Australia and New Guinea

Habitat: Open forests, fields, and agricultural areas

Diet: Small mammals, reptiles, and small birds

FUN FACT
Nankeen is a type of reddish-brown cloth that was popular in the 1700s and 1800s. The nankeen kestrel was given its name because its color is similar.

ROCK KESTREL *(FALCO RUPICOLUS)*

Rock kestrels are often seen in rocky, open areas. They spend a lot of time in the air as they hover in search for large insects and reptiles. Rock kestrels are reddish brown with darker streaks or stripes. They have gray heads. Rock kestrels also have yellow feet and yellow rings around their eyes.

HOW TO SPOT

Size: 10.5 to 14 inches (27 to 36 cm) long; 0.22 to 0.7 pounds (0.1 to 0.3 kg)

Range: Southern Africa

Habitat: Open forests, grasslands, steppes, deserts, coasts, and mountains

Diet: Large insects and reptiles

WHAT ARE KESTRELS?

Kestrels are a group of small falcons that share the same hunting style. Instead of soaring or perching like other raptors, kestrels hunt by hovering above the ground. Then they swoop down on unsuspecting prey.

OSPREY *(PANDION HALIAETUS)*

Among raptors, ospreys are unusual because they feed mainly on live fish. In fact, up to 99 percent of their diet is fish. Ospreys dive feet-first to catch fish in the water. The tiny spikes on the bottoms of their feet and reversible outer toes help them grasp their slippery prey. The osprey is a large bird with a chocolate-brown back and wings. It has a white belly and legs. Its white head has black markings extending from its eyes, and there is a small crest on the back of its head.

HOW TO SPOT

Size: 21 to 23 inches (53 to 58 cm) long; 3 to 4.5 pounds (1.4 to 2 kg)

Range: Africa, Asia, Australia, Europe, North America, Central America, and South America

Habitat: Forests, rivers, lakes, estuaries, and coasts

Diet: Fish

SECRETARY BIRD
(SAGITTARIUS SERPENTARIUS)

Unlike most raptors, the crane-like secretary bird prefers to stalk its prey by walking along the ground instead of flying above it. Secretary birds have very long legs and tails. They also have bold color patterns with pale-gray heads and necks, darker-gray wings, and nearly black feathers at the base of their tails and along their upper legs. Secretary birds also have bare, orange-red faces and black, quill-like feathers that grow from the backs of their heads.

FUN FACT
When secretary birds find prey, they subdue it by kicking the prey with their powerful feet and legs.

HOW TO SPOT

Size: 50 to 60 inches (127 to 152 cm) long; 5 to 9 pounds (2.3 to 4.1 kg)
Range: Africa
Habitat: Savannas and steppes
Diet: Grasshoppers, beetles, and small reptiles including lizards

BARRED OWL *(STRIX VARIA)*

The barred owl is a very vocal bird that makes a range of sounds. It cackles and caws, and its most common call is a series of hoots that sound like "who-cooks-for-you, who-cooks-for-you-all." Barred owls are stocky birds. They have large, round heads; forward-facing, dark eyes; and yellow beaks. Their bodies are brown and white with various streaks and spots.

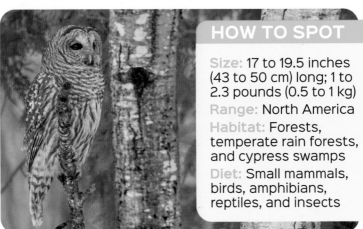

HOW TO SPOT

Size: 17 to 19.5 inches (43 to 50 cm) long; 1 to 2.3 pounds (0.5 to 1 kg)

Range: North America

Habitat: Forests, temperate rain forests, and cypress swamps

Diet: Small mammals, birds, amphibians, reptiles, and insects

BLAKISTON'S FISH OWL
(KETUPA BLAKISTONI)

The Blakiston's fish owl is the biggest owl species in the world. It can weigh up to 10 pounds (4.5 kg) and has an incredible 6-foot (1.8-m) wingspan. These birds have long, brown feathers that look like shaggy fur. They also have dramatic ear tufts that look like ears. Unlike other owls, they're not silent flyers. That doesn't matter much, though, because their main prey is fish.

HOW TO SPOT

Size: 23 to 28 inches (58 to 71 cm) long; 7 to 10 pounds (3.2 to 4.5 kg)
Range: Japan, Russia, and China
Habitat: Old-growth forests near rivers and coasts
Diet: Fish, crustaceans, birds, and frogs

FUN FACT
Male and female Blakiston's fish owls perform their calls in a duet.

AN ENDANGERED OWL

Blakiston's fish owls are endangered. They live only in a few remote areas of old-growth forests in China, Japan, and far-eastern Russia. They tend to avoid contact with people.

BOREAL OWL *(AEGOLIUS FUNEREUS)*

The boreal owl is a small, compact owl with a rounded, flat-topped head. Its face is white, while its head and wings are brown with white spots. Its underside is streaked white and brown. The boreal owl's range is circumpolar, meaning that it lives in the areas of the world that surround the north pole. These owls prefer to live in forests and typically nest in tree cavities.

HOW TO SPOT

Size: 8.5 to 11 inches (22 to 28 cm) long; 0.2 to 0.5 pounds (0.09 to 0.23 kg)

Range: Northern areas of Asia, Europe, and North America

Habitat: Boreal and subalpine forests

Diet: Small mammals, birds, and insects

BURROWING OWL
(ATHENE CUNICULARIA)

Most owl species nest in trees, but the burrowing owl creates its nest underground. These small, long-legged owls are found in open areas where they can lay their eggs in the abandoned burrows of other animals, such as ground squirrels and armadillos. Burrowing owls have small, rounded heads; short tails; and long, pale legs. Their feathers are brown and white, alternating with streaks and spots.

HOW TO SPOT

Size: 9 to 10 inches (23 to 25 cm) long; 0.3 to 0.6 pounds (0.13 to 0.25 kg)

Range: North America, Central America, and South America

Habitat: Grasslands, steppes, airports, farm fields, and golf courses

Diet: Insects, small mammals, reptiles, and birds

FUN FACT
Although burrowing owls can fly, they're often seen hunting for prey by hopping or running on the ground.

CRESTED OWL *(LOPHOSTRIX CRISTATA)*

The crested owl makes its home in the dense, tropical forests of Central and South America. It mainly eats large insects such as beetles and caterpillars. Crested owls have a unique and unmistakable appearance. While their bodies are various shades of brown and white, they have dramatic, white eyebrows that extend into long ear tufts.

HOW TO SPOT

Size: 15 to 17 inches (38 to 43 cm) long; 0.8 to 1.4 pounds (0.4 to 0.6 kg)

Range: Central America and South America

Habitat: Tropical forests

Diet: Large insects

OWL FEATURES

Nearly all owls are nocturnal birds of prey. They share physical features such as forward-facing eyes, a disc-shaped face, excellent eyesight and hearing, and special wing feathers that help them fly quietly or even silently.

ELF OWL *(MICRATHENE WHITNEYI)*

The tiny elf owl is the smallest owl in the world. It lives in dry habitats in Mexico and the southwestern United States, where it nests in tree cavities and inside saguaro cacti. Elf owls have small, rounded heads and are variously streaked and spotted in brown-and-white patterns. They have white markings on their upper wings. Elf owls also have white eyebrows. These birds get preyed on by a variety of species, such as great horned owls and Mexican jays. When a predator is near, elf owls group together to drive it away.

FUN FACT

The elf owl eats tiny prey, such as moths and crickets. The bird will also eat more threatening creatures such as scorpions.

HOW TO SPOT

Size: 4.5 to 5.5 inches (11 to 14 cm) long; 0.06 to 0.1 pounds (0.03 to 0.05 kg)

Range: Southern North America

Habitat: Deserts and subtropical woodlands

Diet: Moths, beetles, scorpions, and crickets

EURASIAN EAGLE OWL
(BUBO BUBO)

The Eurasian eagle owl is a large and powerful predator. It has a barrel-shaped body, strong talons, and long ear tufts. Despite its large size, this owl is not often seen. It prefers to live in wilderness areas away from humans. Eurasian eagle owls are medium brown with black, vertical streaks throughout their feathers. They're lighter colored underneath and have a white patch on their throats. Eurasian eagle owls usually hunt at night, but when food is scarce they will hunt in the daytime.

HOW TO SPOT

Size: 23 to 28 inches (58 to 71 cm) long; 3 to 9 pounds (1.4 to 4.1 kg)

Range: Asia and Europe

Habitat: Forests, cliffs, ravines, and steppes

Diet: Mammals, amphibians, reptiles, and fish

GREAT GRAY OWL *(STRIX NEBULOSA)*

Great gray owls are experts at hunting rodents, their main food source. They can hear rodents that are hidden under thick snow and break through the snowpack to catch them. Great gray owls have mottled, gray-and-brown bodies and large, rounded heads. A black spot marks the owl's chin, and the owl also has a white collar. Great gray owls have two facial discs. The feathers on these discs form circles around each of the bird's eyes. These feathers move sounds to the owl's ears.

HOW TO SPOT

Size: 24 to 33 inches (61 to 84 cm) long; 2 to 2.5 pounds (0.9 to 1.1 kg)

Range: Asia, Europe, and North America

Habitat: Dense boreal forests

Diet: Rodents

FUN FACT
Great gray owls look incredibly large, but most of their bulk is from a thick layer of feathers.

GREAT HORNED OWL
(BUBO VIRGINIANUS)

Great horned owls are adaptable birds that live in many habitats, including city neighborhoods and parks. The great horned owl is an expert hunter. It eats a wide range of prey, including mammals and birds that can be as large as the owl itself. Great horned owls have large, bulky bodies. They also have ear tufts that look like horns or ears. Their backs are spotted with brown and black coloring, and their undersides are white with black and brown bars. The great horned owl has a white patch on its throat.

HOW TO SPOT

Size: 18 to 25 inches (45 to 64 cm) long; 2.5 to 3.5 pounds (1.1 to 1.6 kg)

Range: North America, Central America, and South America

Habitat: Forests, wetlands, agricultural areas, and suburban and urban areas

Diet: Mammals, birds, amphibians, and reptiles

FUN FACT
People once called the great horned owl the winged tiger or the tiger of the air because it is such a fierce hunter.

LONG-EARED OWL *(ASIO OTUS)*

The forest-dwelling long-eared owl has mottled brown, white, and rust-colored feathers that look like tree bark. These owls have ear tufts and white patches near their eyes that look like eyebrows. They are slender and able to compress their feathers and elongate their ear tufts and bodies. This makes them look similar to the tree branches they perch on. Females are typically bigger than males and often have darker coloring.

HOW TO SPOT

Size: 11 to 16 inches (28 to 41 cm) long; 0.5 to 0.9 pounds (0.2 to 0.4 kg)

Range: Africa, Asia, Europe, and North America

Habitat: Open forests

Diet: Small rodents and birds

NORTHERN HAWK OWL
(SURNIA ULULA)

The northern hawk owl is different from most owls in two main ways. First, it's active during the day rather than at night. Second, it isn't wary of humans. Northern hawk owls, however, are rarely seen or studied because they live in remote areas of the northern hemisphere. The northern hawk owl has white spots on top of dark, chocolate coloring. Its underside is a cream color with horizontal, reddish-brown bars. The sides of its gray face are outlined in dark brown. The northern hawk owl has a long tail and short, pointed wings.

HOW TO SPOT

Size: 14 to 17 inches (36 to 43 cm) long; 0.6 to 0.8 pounds (0.3 to 0.4 kg)

Range: Asia, Europe, and North America

Habitat: Forests, parks, and roadsides

Diet: Small mammals and small birds

NORTHERN SAW-WHET OWL
(AEGOLIUS ACADICUS)

Northern saw-whet owls are common throughout their range. However, they can be difficult to see, because they are small and secretive birds that are strictly nocturnal. Northern saw-whet owls are compact birds with round heads, short tails, and rounded wings. Except for their pale-brown wings, they're mostly white with pale-brown markings. They have large eyes.

HOW TO SPOT

Size: 7 to 8.5 inches (18 to 22 cm) long; 0.16 to 0.22 pounds (0.07 to 0.1 kg)

Range: North America

Habitat: Forests, wetlands, and bogs

Diet: Rodents, birds, and insects

FUN FACT

The northern saw-whet owl got its common name from the sound it makes. People thought its call sounded like a saw being scraped against a whetstone, a tool used for sharpening objects.

PHARAOH EAGLE-OWL
(BUBO ASCALAPHUS)

The pharaoh eagle-owl is found in desert or dry habitats in northern Africa and parts of the Arabian Peninsula. Pharaoh eagle-owls like to roost and nest on cliffs, in crevices, and sometimes among rocks on the ground. The pharaoh eagle-owl is a large owl that has barred and mottled feathers in various shades of brown, black, and white. Its face has white markings and a dark outline.

HOW TO SPOT

Size: 17 to 20 inches (43 to 51 cm) long; 4 to 5 pounds (1.8 to 2.3 kg)

Range: Northern Africa and the Middle East

Habitat: Mountains, rocky desert hills, and dry savannas

Diet: Small mammals, birds, and reptiles

SNOWY OWL *(BUBO SCANDIACUS)*

Snowy owls live and nest farther north than any other owl. For much of the year they live on the Arctic tundra, where they build mounded nests on the ground and hunt lemmings, which are small rodents. Male snowy owls are almost entirely white. Female snowy owls are white with dark barring on their heads, wings, and undersides. Both male and female snowy owls have feathered legs. Snowy owls migrate to where they can find prey and will breed more often when food is abundant.

HOW TO SPOT

Size: 20 to 27 inches (51 to 69 cm) long; 3.5 to 6.5 pounds (1.6 to 2.9 kg)
Range: Northern Asia, Europe, and North America
Habitat: Tundra, farm fields, and marshes
Diet: Birds and small mammals such as lemmings

Female

FUN FACT

Snowy owls are very territorial. They are even known to defend their nests from Arctic foxes.

SPOTTED OWL *(STRIX OCCIDENTALIS)*

The spotted owl is one of the owl species that is most threatened by human activities. That's because it lives in old-growth forests in North America that are often logged. Spotted owls need these dense, shaded forests for nesting, roosting, and hunting. The spotted owl is brown with white spots over most of its body.

FUN FACT
When feeding their young, spotted owls tear off the prey's head before giving the body to their owlets. The adult eats the head.

HOW TO SPOT

Size: 18 to 19 inches (46 to 48 cm) long; 1 to 1.75 pounds (0.5 to 0.8 kg)
Range: North America
Habitat: Old-growth forests
Diet: Rodents and other small mammals

TAWNY OWL *(STRIX ALUCO)*

Tawny owls are medium-sized owls with large, rounded heads. Their feathers tend to be reddish brown or gray with streaks of white and darker brown. Tawny owls' faces are outlined with darker rings of feathers. This species lives in forests or areas that have large trees where they can roost and nest. Tawny owls watch for prey while sitting in trees. Then they glide silently toward the prey and kill it with their claws, though sometimes the owls will snap the prey's neck with their beaks. Tawny owls also use their wings to scare other birds out of brush and will then pursue the birds in the air.

HOW TO SPOT

Size: 14.5 to 15 inches (37 to 38 cm) long; 0.9 to 1.1 pounds (0.4 to 0.5 kg)

Range: Asia and Europe

Habitat: Forests, suburban and urban parks, and farm fields

Diet: Small mammals, birds, and insects

AUSTRALASIAN GRASS OWL
(TYTO LONGIMEMBRIS)

Australasian grass owls hunt prey by flying low over grassy areas at night, using their eyes and ears to detect rodents and other small animals. These owls have pale, heart-shaped faces. Their bellies and the undersides of their wings are mainly white. Australasian grass owls have various shades of brown colorings on their wings with white spots.

HOW TO SPOT

Size: 12.5 to 15 inches (32 to 38 cm) long; 0.5 to 1.25 pounds (0.2 to 0.57 kg)
Range: Asia and Australia
Habitat: Grasslands, savannas, and agricultural areas
Diet: Small mammals, birds, and insects

AUSTRALIAN MASKED OWL
(TYTO NOVAEHOLLANDIAE)

The Australian masked owl is a species of barn owl that lives only in certain coastal regions of Australia. Like other barn owls, it has a slightly heart-shaped face that directs sound toward its ears. Australian masked owls appear in three different colors called morphs: pale, intermediate, and dark. No matter the color, the shading pattern is the same. All Australian masked owls have pale faces and undersides with darker wings and backs.

HOW TO SPOT

Size: 13 to 18.5 inches (33 to 47 cm) long; 0.9 to 3 pounds (0.4 to 1.3 kg)
Range: Australia
Habitat: Open forests
Diet: Mammals, birds, and insects

FUN FACT
In some parts of Australia, Australian masked owls roost in caves. Some people call them cave owls because of this.

BARN OWL *(TYTO ALBA)*

True to its name, the barn owl likes to nest in barns and empty buildings. It has one of the widest geographical ranges of any bird species. The barn owl has small, dark eyes and a white face surrounded by a short ruff of feathers. It has a white underside and long, feathered legs. The bird's head and back are often golden to reddish brown with gray-and-black spots and streaks. Its wings are rounded, and the owl has a short tail. Females are larger and longer than males.

HOW TO SPOT

Size: 12.5 to 15.5 inches (32 to 39 cm) long; 0.8 to 1.6 pounds (0.4 to 0.7 kg)

Range: Africa, Asia, Australia, Europe, North America, Central America, and South America

Habitat: Grasslands, marshes, agricultural areas, cliffs, and suburban and urban areas

Diet: Small mammals

FUN FACT

The barn owl has such good hearing that it can locate and strike prey even in total darkness.

BARN OWL OFFSPRING

Barn owls have a relatively short lifespan—around two years. That means they get to breed and raise young only once or twice in their lives. A female lays an average of four to seven eggs and spends most of her time at the nest. Her male partner brings her food. When the eggs hatch, the female is the only one that feeds the offspring. She rips apart food from the male and feeds the chicks tiny pieces of it.

GREATER SOOTY OWL
(TYTO TENEBRICOSA)

The greater sooty owl makes its home in the lush rain forests of eastern Australia, where it roosts in the canopy. This is also where it hunts tree-dwelling mammals such as ringtail possums. The greater sooty owl is black to dark gray overall with silvery spots. Its face, underside, and feathered legs are lighter brown, gray, or white. Greater sooty owls also have dark eyes, short wings, and feet that seem too big for their bodies.

HOW TO SPOT

Size: 14.5 to 17 inches (37 to 43 cm) long; 1 to 2 pounds (0.5 to 0.9 kg)
Range: Australia
Habitat: Rain forests
Diet: Mammals

GLOSSARY

barred
To have alternate bands with different colors.

carrion
The flesh and bones of a dead animal.

deciduous
Trees that drop their leaves at least once a year, often in the fall or winter.

down feathers
Soft layers of feathers near a bird's skin.

ear tufts
Groups of longer feathers on a bird's head that resemble ears.

estuaries
Areas where freshwater rivers or streams meet the salty ocean.

mottled
To have blotches of two colors or more.

prey
An animal that's taken by another for food.

raptor
A medium to large carnivorous bird with sharp claws and a hooked beak.

scavenge
To search for carrion to feed on.

steppes
Large areas of flat, treeless land.

talons
Claws.

vertebrate
An animal with a backbone.

TO LEARN MORE

FURTHER READINGS

Abell, Tracy. *Birds*. Abdo, 2021.

Burnie, David. *Eagle and Birds of Prey*. DK, 2016.

Mikkola, Heimo. *Owls of the World: A Photographic Guide*. Firefly, 2019.

ONLINE RESOURCES

To learn more about birds of prey, please visit **abdobooklinks.com** or scan this QR code. These links are routinely monitored and updated to provide the most current information available.

PHOTO CREDITS

ABDOBOOKS.COM

Published by Abdo Publishing, a division of ABDO, PO Box 398166, Minneapolis, Minnesota 55439. Copyright © 2023 by Abdo Consulting Group, Inc. International copyrights reserved in all countries. No part of this book may be reproduced in any form without written permission from the publisher. Abdo Reference™ is a trademark and logo of Abdo Publishing.

Printed in the United States of America, North Mankato, Minnesota.
052022
092022

Editor: Alyssa Sorenson
Series Designer: Colleen McLaren
Content Consultant: Stephen Pruett-Jones, PhD, associate professor of ecology and evolution, University of Chicago

Library of Congress Control Number: 2021952334
Publisher's Cataloging-in-Publication Data
Names: Debbink, Andrea, author.
Title: Birds of prey / by Andrea Debbink
Description: Minneapolis, Minnesota: Abdo Publishing, 2023 | Series: Field guides | Includes online resources and index.
Identifiers: ISBN 9781532198809 (lib. bdg.) | ISBN 9781098272456 (ebook)
Subjects: LCSH: Birds--Juvenile literature. | Birds of prey--Juvenile literature. | Birds--Behavior—Juvenile literature. | Animals--Identification--Juvenile literature. | Zoology--Juvenile literature.
Classification: DDC 598.2--dc23